HOW GREAT A FLAME

Contemporary Lessons
from the Wesleyan Revival

James C. Logan

GBOD

EQUIPPING WORLD-CHANGING DISCIPLES

www.gbod.org
PO Box 340003
Nashville, TN 37203-0003

"Evangelism is not an optional activity of the church; it is an expression of the church's very being and mission."

❧ James C. Logan

Interior layout: Steven W. Manskar

ISBN 0-88177-472-3

Library of Congress Control Number 2005921236

DR 472

Contents

Foreword

To paraphrase the opening sentence of Leo Tolstoy's novel *Anna Karenina*: Healthy churches are all alike; every unhealthy church is unhealthy in its own way. James Logan helps us see the disease within ourselves and within our church when we make separate that which Mr. Wesley and Jesus Christ joined together—vital piety and social witness.

Two prongs of our understanding of Christian discipleship are known as *vital piety* and *social witness*. We see vital piety and social witness entwined in churches as they reach out to others in evangelism, and as they reach out to bear witness to compassion, justice, and mercy.

For Mr. Wesley, vital piety was essential. Daily Scripture reading and prayer was expected. Participation in weekly meetings with others for accountability, and attendance at worship and the Lord's Supper were essential. These practices informed the faith and witness of Mr. Wesley and drove him out of the doors of the Church to the streets, where he preached and invited others, through evangelical zeal, to receive the gift of faith in Christ.

Yet, Mr. Wesley's understanding of Christian discipleship did not end with the profession of faith and commitment of new life in Jesus Christ. He expected growth in faith that would send faithful people into the world to address the social issues of the day—poverty, hunger, and injustice of every form. His social witness did not follow from a mild concern for others. Rather, it sprang from the depths of his understanding of what it means to love God and others. Wesley talked with his preachers about "doing no harm and doing good." He expected that perspective to energize the Methodists of his day.

In the church of today, these two are often divided—as if Christian disciples are called only to lives of piety or only to social witness. We sometimes see church people fight with one another; with one side emphasizing vital piety and the other focusing on social witness.

James Logan offers a thought-provoking book that explores the essential connection between vital piety and social witness among the 18th century Wesleyan revial. Logan gives us details from the life of Martha Thompson, who came to Christ through hearing the preaching of John Wesley. She was subsequently committed to the notorious mental institution at Bedlam. While there she organized a Methodist class meeting. Martha was released from Bedlam and continued her ministry to sick and poor people. If Dr. Logan gave us only Martha's story, we would be inspired. But he helps us move from the 18th century into the 21st century by challenging our understanding of evangelism.

In the late 1800s Methodists in the United States of America were primary participants in the building of many institutions that we now recognize as vital to a healthy society. They built schools, hospitals, clinics, colleges, universities, and orphanages. Methodists in those days saw clearly the link between social witness and vital piety. The two were inseparable expressions of what it means to love God and to love the neighbor as oneself.

This United Methodists ethos continues today as people across the world build similar institutions in various countries. In those places if you ask, "Where are the United Methodists?" the answer will be "Oh, they are working in a local clinic, child advocacy network, or homeless shelter." The examples of United Methodists who are linking social witness and vital piety are legion. In many places across the world, all you have to do is to ask, "Where are they?" Examples of faithful people at work are all around us.

There are some people who describe us as "the do-gooder" crowd. Yet, we know in our hearts that we do our work of ministry because of who we are. John Wesley was clear to say that our duty was to "do no harm, do good, and practice the works of piety. The linkage between these three was inseparable. To be a Methodist meant that one could not do one without the others. Paying deep attention to the disciplines and practices of faith (Bible reading, worship, the Lord's Supper, & fasting) was expected. Methodists were held accountable for these practices in the class meetings. They knew that practicing these disciplines was never enough. They had to live their faith in the world to make a difference; to bring justice and compassion to bear in all places. Why? Wesley's answer was "to flee from the wrath to come." There was an urgency and necessity for response to Christ and his amazing grace. God would hold Methodists accountable for who they were and what they did. Mr. Wesley was very clear about that reality, and so should we be today!

Thus, Dr. Logan links vital piety and social witness in such a way that we see the passion of the early Methodists. Our hearts and minds are warmed as we recognize ourselves within the pages of this book. We are reminded that our love and passion for following Jesus Christ moves us to go more deeply into the life of faith, and to live faithfully and fruitfully in our witness and work with Christ in the world.

We who live within the Wesleyan tradition offer a gift to the larger Christian community and to the world. We clearly understand the interconnectedness of vital piety and social witness. James Logan reminds us that this linkage is unbreakable, if we are faithful to our Wesleyan theology, polity, and practice.

As you read this book, consider the ways in which you, and your church, can reach out to others more effectively as you witness to a faith in Jesus Christ that joins a piety that is vibrant and vital with a witness that extends to the depths of the sorrows and injustices of the world.

Rev. Karen Greenwaldt
General Secretary
The General Board of Discipleship
The United Methodist Church

CHAPTER ONE

How Great a Flame

The scene was one of those indescribably quaint Cotswold villages perched on the border of Gloucestershire and Oxfordshire. I strolled down the main street lined with those ancient dwellings built so durably with the Cotswold pinkish gray stone and topped with the weathered red tile roofs. Suddenly my attention was arrested with the sight of a small, architecturally nondescript Methodist chapel, its severe lines in sharp contrast to the other structures.

The chapel door ushered one directly into the preaching room (apparently British Methodists in the late nineteenth century had not discovered the narthex!). On the back wall of the chapel I noticed three familiar prints of Victorian etchings of imagined scenes from the life of

John Wesley. Many Methodist chapels are adorned with these reproductions, and the scenes are always the same.

One print was of the Epworth rectory fire of 1709 with little "Jackie" being lowered from the upstairs window while the billows of flame and smoke engulfed the house. How many Methodists have looked upon that picture and recalled the reputed words of Susanna, "Behold, a brand plucked from the burning."[1]

The second picture took us to Oxford sometime between the years of 1726 and 1729. In 1725 John Wesley had been elected a fellow of Lincoln College. Almost immediately he slipped off to Epworth where his ailing father needed his assistance, particularly with the little adjunct parish church of Wroote. The principal of Lincoln summoned John back to Oxford to fulfill his responsibilities as tutor. Charles had arrived in Oxford from London to begin his university studies, and John discovered a loosely knit group gathered around Charles seeking a more serious practice of the Christian life. One thing the group lacked greatly, and that was systematic organization—a task for which John, in contrast to Charles, was admirably suited. The result was the Holy Club. Here on the walls of this little chapel was an imagined scene of the Holy Club meeting in some student chamber, possibly at Christ Church.

The third print took us to London in the year 1791—the year of Wesley's death. The scene was Wesley lying on his deathbed, and the viewer was undoubtedly expected to recall the words, "The best of all is, God is with us."

If American Methodists were to have made an addition to this picture gallery, they would unquestionably have submitted a picture of Wesley at Aldersgate Street, London, 1738. More than our British sisters and brothers, we American Methodists have had a fascination with Wesley's "warmed heart" at Aldersgate Street. In fact, for many years we carried a description of this scene in our *Disciplines,* a depiction that depended more upon our imagination than the brief mention of this night in Wesley's *Journal.* We are the children of the Second Great Awakening, and we have sought to include Wesley in this tradition.

Before us now is a gallery of scenes and dates:

- Epworth – 1709
- Oxford – 1729
- London, Aldersgate Street – 1738
- London, City Road – 1791

It is as though a single date or a combination of all four can explain the crucial significance of Wesley for the people called Methodists.

As I viewed this display of prints, I managed to suppress a scream. Something was missing! This chapel would not have been here in this little Cotswold village, and a people called Methodists would not be around today if it had not been for Bristol, April 2, 1739. As important as these other pictures are, something happened in Bristol that should be reckoned as the most important event of all. And so begins a story.

Centering in Bristol and spreading outward George Whitefield was already creating his own chapter in the history of the eighteenth century evangelical revival. He was moving out of the parish churches and preaching in the marketplaces and open fields to masses of people. In 1739 Whitefield was preparing for a preaching mission to Wales, from whence he would go on to the American colonies. He urgently summoned his old Oxford companion from the Holy Club, John Wesley, to Bristol "to hold the fort" while he was absent.

Wesley had already heard the reports of Whitefield's unorthodox method of preaching in the open-air, and he had his strong reservations. Of Whitefield's invitation to Bristol, Wesley wrote in his Journal: "I was fully employed between our own Society in Fetter Lane and many others, when I received a letter from Mr. Whitefield, entreating me in the most pressing manner to come to Bristol without delay. *This I was not at all forward to do.*"[2]

In addition to questioning the propriety of Whitefield's method, John had additional reasons, so he thought, to stay away from Bristol. His brother Charles was "extremely averse" to what Whitefield was doing. Furthermore, John thought he was going to die (a constant preoccupation throughout his life). The Fetter Lane

Society resorted to the ancient method of determination by casting lots. The lot favored Whitefield, and this curious Scripture passage is one of those drawn and quoted as favoring Bristol: "Now there was a long war between the house of Saul and the house of David; but David waxed stronger and stronger, and the house of Saul waxed weaker and weaker." Fetter Lane's interpretation was that Whitefield and John stood for David the stronger, and Charles and Fetter Lane stood for Saul the weaker. Wesley set out for Bristol the next day.

John Wesley arrived in Bristol on Saturday, March 31. On that day he would have observed the river full of sailing vessels, some of them the slave ships of Bristol owners. Bristol, the river port, was the financial center of the trans-Atlantic slave trade. The narrow rutty streets of the old "walled-in" section of the city would have been alive with seamen let loose among the crowds of Bristol natives. These seamen, having been "cooped up" on board for weeks, would have been hungry for the excitement offered by prostitution and the ever present alehouses. It was not a pretty sight!

April 1, 1739, was the day of great discovery for John Wesley. On this day, he saw his friend Whitefield at his greatest and best, reveling in the glorious opportunities God had given him, preaching to vast congregations at the Bowling Green, Hanham, and Rose Garden.

Wesley wrote in his *Journal*, "I could scarce reconcile myself at first to this strange way of preaching in the fields, of which he set me an example on Sunday, having been all my life (till very lately) so tenacious of every point relating to decency and order, that I should have thought the saving of souls almost a sin if it had not been done in a church."[3] Note the phrase, *I could scarce reconcile myself*—that is the preamble to his venture in open-air preaching. And at the end of his days, he still spoke of open-air preaching as "a cross."

To speak the truth, we modern Methodists are to this extent with Wesley. We are as sensitive to respectability, decency, and order as was Wesley. For over a century we have left the street corners to the Salvation Army. In a therapeutic culture we have reduced the gospel of salvation to inspiration leading to self-help. In a technological age we have left television to charlatans masquerading as evangelists. We have allowed our churches to become bogged down in an intramural squabble over new forms of worship. Wesley's words could just as easily be ours—*I could scarce reconcile myself.*

But herein lies the difference between Wesley and us. It was "the cross" he chose to bear, and the one which we leave to other churches and groups who don't conform to our standards of decency and order. The next day, April 2, 1739, is the first of days, the date of the first Methodist popular assembly. Wesley wrote, "At four in the afternoon, *I submitted to be more vile* (2 Sam 6:22) and proclaimed in the highways the glad tidings of salvation, speaking from a little eminence in a ground adjoining the city to about three thousand people. The scripture on which I spoke was this (is it possible that any one should be ignorant that it is fulfilled in every true minister of Christ?)—"The Spirit of the Lord is upon us because he hath anointed me to preaching the Gospel to the poor . . ."[4] This is the same text that he had expounded on board the *Simmonds* on his way to Georgia. But something was different now. Now in his exposition there was soul-deliverance, newness of life, and an exultation he had not known before. And the people soon knew it too. So much so that the *Cambridge Modern History* declares, "From this day, April 2, 1739, may be reckoned a new era in the religious history of England; for her greatest religious leader between Cromwell and Newman had found his way to the hearts of her people."[5]

The first Sunday after Whitefield left him in charge at Bristol, Wesley estimated that he had about seventy-five thousand at his open-air services, and the following Sunday, fourteen thousand. Wesley stated that the recorded numbers were reached "by computation," though he did not give his formula for such. At a later time, he estimated that about seven persons could stand within one square yard. Such calculations depended upon the accuracy of his judgment of what constituted one square yard! Wesley recorded the attendance at his field preaching during this first month in the Bristol area as totaling approximately fifty thousand, which would average to slightly more than three thousand per preaching event. This was within five weeks of the time when he said he could scarce reconcile himself to the strange new way. Whatever one says about Wesley's unscientific methods of calculation, in any event the crowds were spectacularly large. Not as large as Whitefield's crowds (Wesley did not have the homiletical powers of a Whitefield); nevertheless the crowds were large by any standard of measurement.

Traveling back and forth between Bristol and London he records preaching to crowds as great as fifteen thousand at Blackheath and Kennington Common. Charles was something of a skeptic regarding this strange new practice of open-air preaching, and he even questioned the reported numbers. Maybe the reports had been inflated! This was, until John preached at Moorfields on June 24, 1739, where he records a crowd of ten thousand. After that Charles' doubts subsided. By September, John was preaching to crowds in and around London that ranged from twelve to twenty thousand. Wesley had indeed embarked upon a strange new way.

Yet, God's way often is strange; and in this strange way Wesley opened the floodgates of divine mercy. Before the many thousands came to the waters of salvation, those waters came to them. This is evidence of what John called "prevenient grace." He went on this way for fifty years, and in the very year before he died he was still exclaiming, "Come, let us strike a few more blows at the Devil's kingdom."

So open-air preaching was in place as the first component of what would become a significantly different pattern of revival than had previously been known. Wesley journeyed up and down England, and into Wales, Scotland, and Ireland, journeys that were to cease only at his death. Newcastle upon Tyne was the first city of the north of England to be visited, and the triangle of Bristol, London, and Newcastle formed a convenient ground plan for the development of his strategy.

Even more impressive than the reported numbers of the crowds were the testimonies of and narratives about persons. Through Wesley's and his assistants' preaching, combined with the class meetings, people came to know the claims of the grace of Christ upon their lives. Most of these persons we do not know by name. From Wesley's *Journal* and the collected *Letters* we have some fleeting glimpses of persons whom we can know by name. From old copies of *The Arminian Magazine* and from the annals of local societies and chapels we know some of these persons and their stories of faith. I share only one such story. It is illustrative both of the power of Wesley's preaching and the incalculable value of the class meeting.

Martha Thompson's story is particularly insightful because it focuses upon the evangelical experience of a laywoman who came to play a regionally important role in the Wesleyan movement. Wesley's *Journal* mentions Martha Thompson, the first Methodist of Preston in northern Lancastershire because he visited Preston and Martha four times in the decade preceding his death. An obituary appears in *The Arminian Magazine*, and it should be noted that such obituaries were the experiential life stories of persons, stories shared for the spiritual edification of the readers.

Martha Thompson was born of humble means in Preston in 1731. Unlike many young women of her time, she had been schooled in the basic skills of reading and writing. She had also been trained as an apprentice to a tailor. At the age of nineteen, she left Preston and journeyed 209 miles to London where she had obtained a position in the mansion of a wealthy Preston lady.

One day she was sent on an errand to the heart of London and passed Moorfields. There, to her amazement, she saw an enormous crowd, and heard the thousands burst into song. She had never heard such singing before. The preacher was a small man, thin, with fine, shapely cut features and closely shaved chin. He wore a clergyman's gown and bands. He stood on a table, and with an air of calm authority, arrested universal attention.

It was indeed a motley crowd from streets and slums—merchants and tradesmen, outcast and thieves, high born and low born, warm friends and bitter opponents, well-dressed people, ragged and dirty people, and they were all listening. The message was, "Ye must be born again."

Martha was first curious, and then she was spellbound and riveted, and knew not how to tear herself away. Back home her mistress admonished her. "Never listen to that man again. If you do, he will drive you mad, he will ruin you, body and soul." But Martha could not forget.

On several occasions she slipped back to Moorfields to hear the man whom Oxford cynics had called "a little crackbrained." After hearing Wesley one day, during the singing of Isaac Watts' "The Lord Jehovah Reigns," Martha found that inner peace and joy which Wesley called "the inner witness of the Spirit." Watts' words were Martha's deepest feelings:

> And will this sovereign King
> Of glory condescend,
> And will he write his name,
> My Father and my Friend?
> I love his name, I love his word;
> Join all my powers to praise the Lord.[6]

And praise the Lord she did when she returned to the suburban London mansion. "Martha's demented," the servants complained to their mistress. An order was issued that Martha should be admitted to the dreaded institution of Bedlam.

Wesley's request to preach at Bedlam had been rejected. In the *Journal* he wrote, "I have been forbidden to go to Newgate for fear of making them wicked, and now I am forbidden to go to Bedlam for fear of driving them mad." He sent two doctors in his place. Through the doctors Martha was eventually released and found herself back in Preston, a place where there were no Methodists and, indeed, Methodists were despised. She discovered a Methodist class of fifteen members, six miles away out on the moorlands. So every Sunday she walked six miles out and six miles back. By 1759 Martha had gathered a little class of five Methodists in Preston.

Martha Thompson wrote to Wesley, inviting him to come to Preston and visit with her little class meeting. Wesley's first visit to Preston was in 1780. Over the following decade he came to Preston on three other occasions and was guest in Martha's home.

Martha visited the sick, she ministered to the poor, and was ever an "angel of light" among her own people. She lived to be eighty-nine, and when infirm, with a lantern in her hand, a child would lead her in winter to the early morning service and the night service as well. When she came to die, her children and grandchildren gathered round her bed and said, "Let us sing dear old granny home." What did they sing? What else could they sing than the old conversion hymn sung on the occasion of Martha's conversion after having heard Wesley preach? And the last sound she heard on earth was this:

> And will this sovereign King
> Of glory condescend,
> And will he write his name,
> My Father and my Friend?
> I love his name, I love his word;
> Join all my powers to praise the Lord.

Twenty years after Wesley's death, Martha died.

Martha may not have had the facility with words that Wesley had. She did know profoundly, however, in her inner being, the key words of Wesley's preaching—

justification and sanctification. She knew herself to have been pardoned by a Father and a Friend. She knew herself to have been given a new birth in Christ Jesus through the Holy Spirit. She knew the empowering, sanctifying grace through the Holy Spirit. "My Father and My Friend." For Martha this was the essence of the gospel. And this because a young woman once heard by chance—or was it not the prevenient grace of Christ—at Moorfields a slight little man proclaim that very word of grace.[7]

Discussion Questions

1. The phrase, "I could scarce reconcile myself," referred to John Wesley's initial reluctance to accept George Whitefield's invitation to preach at Bristol. What were Wesley's reservations about accepting this invitation to preach?

2. What compelled Wesley to overcome his reservations and become "more vile"?

3. What personal reservations do you struggle with regarding outreach and personal faith sharing?

4. What have you learned about overcoming personal reservations from John Wesley's example?

NOTES

1. There is no recorded account of Susanna having uttered the words and the first recordings of such were in some nineteenth century biographies.

2. *Journal* 2:37.

3. Journal, 2:46.

4. Journal 2:46.

5. *Cambridge Modern History,* VI:83.

6. "The Lord Jehovah Reigns" Isaac Watts, 1709.

7. Martha Thompson's story is recorded in the following: John Taylor, *The Apostles of Fylde Methodism* (London: T. Woolman, 1885), pp. 8-17; J. W. Laycock, *Methodism and Heroes of the Great Haworth Round, 1734-1784* (Keighsey: Wadsworth, Rydal Press, 1909), pp. 198-200; W. Pilkington, *The Makers of Wesleyan Methodism in Preston* (London: Charles H. Kelly, 1890), p. 14; W. F. Richardson, *Preston Methodism's Two Hundred Years* (Preston: Printed at Adelphi Chambers by Henry L. Kirby, 1975), pp. 9-15; Maldwyn Edwards, *My Dear Sister: The Story of John Wesley and the Women in His Life* (Manchester: Periwork (Leeds), n.d.); T. Ferrier Hulme, *Voices of the New Room* (New York: Abingdon Press, 1931), pp. 35-47; Paul Wesley Chilcote, *John Wesley and the Women Preachers of Early Methodism* (Metuchen, NJ: Scarecrow Press, Inc., 1991), p. 50.

CHAPTER TWO

Anatomy of Revival

As a seminary professor I both listen to and preach sermons. On Aldersgate Sunday some years ago I heard a sermon on the Wesleyan heritage. The preacher began the message with this lead sentence, "It began with Wesley." The preacher was well intentioned, but not very well informed.

When Wesley determined to do "that vile thing" and engage in open-air preaching in 1739, the eighteenth century Evangelical Revival was already underway. George Whitefield had begun the para-parish church open-air preaching while Wesley was still in Georgia. In Wales the stirrings of revival were being felt through the preaching of such revivalists Griffith Jones (1682-1761), Howell Harris (1714-73), and Daniel Rowland (1713-80).

Across the Atlantic in 1734, Jonathan Edwards had sparked a revival in Northampton, Massachusetts, with a sermon on justification by faith that eventually converted the entire town of three hundred souls and spread throughout the region. So, Wesley did not originate the Evangelical Revival.

The accounts of the larger eighteenth century Evangelical Revival in no way denigrate nor minimize the importance of the Wesleyan Revival. The Wesleyan Revival had distinctive features that distinguished it from the other expressions of revival. To a considerable extent, these distinctive features, practices, or components explain why the Wesleyan Revival outlasted the others. The Wesleyan Revival stretched across more than fifty years in England, though in the latter decades it showed signs of waning. The American version of the Wesleyan Revival was the most powerful religious force in the New World through the early decades of the nineteenth century.

What were these distinctive features, practices, or components of the Wesleyan Revival? In other words, what was the anatomy of the Wesleyan Revival? We can delineate at least three such practices: open-air preaching (which Wesley held in common with other revivalists such as Whitefield), the organizing of the converts into two distinctive, on-going structures (societies and class meetings), and the deployment of a two-tiered lay ministry (one on the local level consisting of class leaders, exhorters and local preachers, and one on the connectional level of itinerant lay preachers). From 1740 the itinerant lay preachers were organized into an annual conference over which Wesley presided.

One of the chief features of Wesley's revival, which made him distinctively different from other revivalists, was precisely his penchant for organizing the converts and the lay preachers. Whitefield recognized this and remarked, "Joining in class, he preserved the fruit of his labour. This I neglected and my people are a rope of sand." Where others preached and moved on to new pastures, Wesley preached and lingered long enough to organize his people so that a nurturing and sustaining ministry could be carried on when the itinerant preacher was elsewhere.

Not only did the organizational structure perpetuate the revival for a long period of time, but the way in which Wesley put the pieces together also constituted a remarkably coherent, theologically defensible, experientially vital, and consistent pattern of evangelism in a Wesleyan perspective. Rarely in the history of the Church can be found such an integration of theological message, experiential religion, and systematic structure as one finds in the Wesleyan Revival. We turn to the anatomy of the revival.

Preaching

While Wesley shared with the other revivalists a sense of the temporal and logical priority of preaching, there are distinctive marks of his own preaching found both in his practice and in his directions to his lay preachers. Wesley shared with other revivalists an evangelical understanding of proclamation. The purpose of preaching was to announce the "glad tidings," the "good news" of the saving grace of Christ. Of course, this meant that his biblically based sermons were always evangelically motivated to reach the "unreached" and the "lapsed reached" alike, and to provide pastoral counsel. We will later consider the theological message itself. Here we are concerned with how such was to be done, and on this Wesley had definite convictions.

Wesley structured his annual preachers' conference in a question-answer format. Mr. Wesley asked the questions, and Mr. Wesley supplied the answers after allowing limited discussion. Such organizational procedure prompted Ronald Knox, with some justification, to conclude that Wesley could work only with "Yes men."[1] Two illustrations from the conference of 1744 illustrate the style of conference:

> Q. In what view may the Methodist Preachers be considered?
> A. As messengers sent by the Lord out of the common way to provoke the regular clergy to jealousy (i.e., zeal) and to supply their lack of service towards those who are perishing for want of knowledge and above all to reform the nation by spreading scriptural holiness over the lands.

Wesley's lay preachers had limited education, theological discipline, and professional training. In many instances they were lacking in basic knowledge and skills for what could be considered effective preaching. They nevertheless reached the masses simply ignored by more educated and skilled clergy. On the score of bringing regular clergy to jealousy, these lay preachers were indeed quite effective! One has only to read the many accounts in Wesley's *Journal* of the intrigues to which some clergy went to obstruct Wesley and his lay preachers.

In that same 1744 conference Wesley addressed the matter of what to preach and as was typical of Wesley, he ordered it very systematically:

Q. What is the best general method of preaching?
A. To invite, (2) To convince, (3) To offer Christ,
(4) To build up and to do this (in some measure)
in every sermon.

In one way or another, Wesley endeavored to do this in every sermon. The message was profoundly theological, while being at the same time profoundly simple. William Fitzgerald summarized the message, claiming that against the background of an arid Calvinism, and even more clearly against the apathy and irreligion due to the Deist's philosophy, the faith of the Early Methodists stands out in bold relief. Wesley and his preachers proclaimed:[2]

Wesleyan Proclamation	Doctrine
All need to be saved	Sinful condition
All may be saved	Justification
All may know themselves saved	Assurance
All may be saved to the uttermost	Sanctification

When one moves from the *Journal* to the *Sermons* one can see the logic of Wesley's preaching. While the printed sermons were not in most instances as Wesley actually preached them, one can be certain that congruence exists between Wesley's sermons and his spoken words. Wesley published sermons for pedagogical purposes. They were to be read and inwardly digested by the people. Quite simply, the published sermons were for spiritual edification. Wesley usually preached in an extemporaneous style. Wesley put great value upon logical (and moral) consistency, and it would be difficult for today's interpreter of Wesley to claim otherwise. In terms of content, the extemporaneous sermons were in agreement with the printed sermons.

What was Wesley's intention in preaching? Certainly, the intention was to reach as many people as possible with the gospel and to announce the Good News in a style that was "plain truth for plain people." The gospel as "plain truth for plain people," as practiced by Wesley, carried an inherent logic.

First, the sermon was declarative. To proclaim the "glad tidings" was the way Wesley expressed it in writing about his first Bristol experiences of preaching. The message of "glad tidings" was not a derivative of human experience. It was the announcement of a story of God's action in Jesus Christ. It was a story of Christ's atonement, which in turn interpreted human experience. Only in this sense can we speak of a Wesleyan theology of religious experience. Experience or "heart religion" was critical for Wesley, and "heart religion" was a constant manifestation in revival. But experience did not generate the theology. The gospel message of salvation delivered through Scripture and tradition interpreted the experience. The message does not arise from the experience; it is addressed to the experience and provides people with the opportunity to claim the story and name their experience. The first obligation of the preacher is, therefore, simply to tell the "old, old, story of Jesus and his love." Charles Wesley concisely expressed this intention in these words:

> Our God contracted to a span
> Incomprehensibly made man.[3]

Second, the sermon is descriptive. From the perspective of the declaration of God's action in Christ, Wesley describes the dynamics of the grace of Christ in the life of the Christian. It is not sufficient simply to say that Christ saves us. It is necessary to set forth what that salvation means in the autobiography of the believer.

For Wesley the saving grace of Christ is singular. How could it be otherwise? Christ is the personification, the incarnation, of divine grace. The singular grace of

Christ works in the life of the believer in three principle modes or ways. Wesley attempts to describe this threefold working of grace in the Christian's life. This he understood to be the singular task of practical divinity. Practical divinity is the "mapping" of divine grace in the Christian's experience of salvation. Preveniently, the grace of Christ finds the person, and awakens him or her to the universal human condition of being without God or being over-against God. The first function of grace in the life of the believer is to awaken from slumber and create an awareness of sin, which for the truly awakened person, leads to repentance. Note that grace prompts and makes repentance happen. We may not even be aware of the prevenient working of grace seeking to bring us to repentance and faith. Nevertheless, the prevenient grace of Christ is antecedent to sin. Thus Wesley can say, "No man sins because he has not grace, but because he does not use the grace he hath."[4]

Prevenient grace comes to its triumph in justifying grace. Here the liberating word of grace sets the person free from the bondage of the will to itself. This is quite simply pardon, says Wesley. We are set in a new relationship with God, not through dependence upon our own wills, but in dependence upon the saving will of God. The early Methodists called this "the glorious deliverance."

In the very moment when justification "comes home" to the human heart, the work of sanctifying grace begins a process of growing in grace. This Wesley understood to be the way of holiness. To be certain, we do not make ourselves holy. But through grace we enter into a co-operant relationship with God whereby we increasingly come to have "the mind in us which was in Christ Jesus" and manifest evidences of the renewal of the divine image.

By way of description, Wesley traced the way of grace in the life of the believer. He thus attempted to provide a means whereby persons could identify their experience, name it, and claim it as the "road map" of their spiritual journey. Such was the life of practical divinity, and such was the descriptive task of preaching.

Third, from declaration to description to decision—this is the logic of the sermon. At this point it is important to note that most of the decisions of faith in the Wesleyan Revival were not made in the preaching services, indoors or out. These decisions were made in the class meeting, which explains why Wesley held that the class meeting was the absolutely necessary companion to the sermon.

It was the primary function of the sermon to awaken. The awakened person with new eyes could see the possibility of salvation, the opportunity for conversion, the need for decision. The awakened person was welcomed into a class meeting where under the guidance of a wise class leader the seeker came from conviction to decision, or conversion. It was the responsibility of the preacher to hold before the people the whole picture of grace, which is always invitational and calls for decision.

Class Meetings and Societies

Preaching, as important as it was, did not suffice for a comprehensive ministry of evangelism. Experience convinced Wesley that awakening souls without providing follow-up guidance, nurture, and discipline was playing into the hands of the devil! Thus his standard reply to reports from his preachers about initial responses of conversion was, "Follow the blow! Never encourage the devil by snatching souls from him that you cannot nurture . . . converts without nurture are like stillborn babes."[5]

From the earliest days of the revival the class meeting was an essential, not an elective, alongside preaching. How could it be otherwise? If the purpose of preaching was to awaken persons to their sinful condition, it was necessary that there be some provision whereby these awakened ones by the grace of Christ could come to faith and continue to grow in grace.

Wesley did not possess some master plan beforehand. Rather, he shaped the revival piece by piece as the exigencies of the moment seemed to demand. He structured the revival from the saddle. Albert Outler, quoting from Origen in the Fondren Lectures of 1974, observed that Wesley "plundered the Egyptians."[6] Others have claimed that Wesley was a "sanctified pragmatist."

Certainly the idea for the formation of the societies on the local scene came to him from within his own Anglican Church. Already in 1678 Anthony Horneck, a German who had been educated at Oxford, had begun some small parish-based societies. Wesley would have been familiar with this development because in Epworth, Wesley's father, Samuel, had begun a religious society fully two years before John was born. Three years prior to that, Samuel had published "A Letter Concerning the Religious Societies" in which he urged the need for pastoral care and spiritual growth, and emphasized that religious societies could help achieve both. In fact, Wesley had gone to Georgia in 1735 under the auspices of one of these Anglican societies, The Society for the Promotion of Christian Knowledge.

From the Moravians and other pietists came the influence for bands and classes. Count Zinzendorf had developed small groups for confession of sin and building each other up from the drawing room meetings of Spener the Pietist, meetings that came to be known as "churches within the church." In an address given on July 2, 1747, Zinzendorf said the inspiration for the bands had come from Mary's visit to Elizabeth, mentioned in Luke 1:39-45.

Wesley was what we would call an eclectic. There is nothing wrong with being an eclectic if you know what you are doing. Unlike so much of contemporary evangelism, which is an indiscriminate borrowing from here and there, Wesley had a discerning mind. He sought for structures of revival that would implement the theological message of plenteous grace—prevenient, justifying, and sanctifying. What began as improvisation and borrowings soon became the bone structure of the revival.

Within two days of Wesley's first open-air sermon, Wesley tells us that early " . . . in the evening three women agreed to meet together weekly, and then, later, four young men for the same purpose . . . to confess their faults one to another and pray for another, that they may be healed."[7]

Such small groups Wesley had witnessed at Hernhutt among the Moravians. These were the bands. Bands, as such, had a short existence within the Methodist movement. Yet from this practice sprang the development of a "society" organization as a means of fellowship. In February of 1742, Wesley divided the entire society into classes of twelve members. Each member agreed to contribute a penny a week toward the debt incurred by building the New Room in Bristol, and one person in each class received the money and handed it to the stewards weekly. Wesley thereby discerned the very thing he needed for edifying the Body of Christ. It was as a most providential discovery, for out of this, and as a richer development of it, came the class meeting and the class leader.

Wesley knew how necessary it was that so-called Christian experience should be checked and guided by the Word of God; and by his God-given method of fellowship he kept the lightheaded, uninstructed and simple-hearted ones on right lines. For example, early in 1744 he made this entry into his *Journal*: "I began examining the society and not before it was wanted, for the plague was begun. I found many crying out, 'Faith, faith,' 'believe, believe' but making little account of the fruits of faith, either of holiness, or good works. In a few days they came to themselves, and had a more thorough understanding of the truth as it is in Jesus."[8]

Later in the same year after completing the first conference of preachers in London, he remained to examine the society. In the *Journal* he wrote, "The next week we endeavoured to purge the society of all that did not walk according to the gospel. By this means we reduced the number of members to less than nineteen hundred. But number is a inconsiderable circumstance. May God increase them in faith and love!"[9]

The class meeting was utterly crucial for the conversion process as Wesley understood it. It may come as a surprise to many to discover that while Wesley did not deny the possibility of instantaneous conversion, in his experience most of the conversions were gradual. When those who had heard the message of free, universal grace evidenced a desire "to flee from the wrath to come," they were immediately enrolled in a class where, under the leadership of a lay class leader, they earnestly sought their salvation.

On the American scene with the demise of the class meeting in Methodism (and hence, the loss of the location for a process of conversion), many conversions ceased to be gradual and became instantaneous, immediately following the evangelistic message. This explains the origin of the practice of the altar call, a practice of which Wesley had never heard and obviously had never seen.

In short, when hearers inquired of Wesley, "How can I find this salvation?" Wesley gathered them into small groups to "work out" their salvation "with fear and trembling." Wesley regarded these class meetings as the "sinews" of the revival.

Within Wesley's own lifetime the class meeting came to function in a dual fashion. The class meeting functioned as the means of grace whereby people were "brought to Christ" (justification), where originally the bands were the means of grace whereby people were "kept with Christ" (sanctification). Even within Wesley's own lifetime the band disappeared, and the class meeting came to fulfill both functions (evangelism and nurture, justification and sanctification). The class meeting was the place where people experienced their conversion or justification, while at the same time the class meeting was the place where people were continually built up in grace or sanctification.

The class meeting waned across the nineteenth century in American Methodism, with the exception of African-American Methodism. Within global Methodism it is instructive to see how the class meeting is constitutive of the Korean Methodist congregations. By the end of the nineteenth century, the class meeting had passed out of the *Discipline* of both the Methodist Episcopal and Methodist Episcopal South churches. With the passing of the class meeting, Wesley's children lost one of the major legacies he had bequeathed to them. With the eclipse of the class meeting, Methodists came more and more to accept and practice a truncated form of evangelism that focused exclusively upon a decisionistic, instantaneous conversion. The Methodists simply had no structure to enflesh the scope of Wesley's view of grace—justifying and sanctifying. The eclipse of the class meeting marked a decided decline in the church's sense of being a discipled people. Without the class meeting the major structure for spiritual accountability was lost, and the church compromised its ecclesial identity, exchanging a missional consciousness for an institutional consciousness. Hence, American Methodists emerged from the nineteenth century void of an ecclesiology and clad only with an ecclesiocracy. Evangelism was reduced to concern for generating an "altar experience" without a "discipleship walk." This was an evangelism that claimed to know the Name, but came dangerously close to forgetting the Story.

Lay Ministry

At every level of the revival there was to be found a highly committed, vigorous lay ministry—with one exception. Mr. Wesley shared with no one, ordained or lay (not even his beloved brother Charles nor the saintly John Fletcher, his most gifted theological defender), his position as the authoritative leader of the revival.

However, those who encountered the good news of the gospel and who were subsequently drawn into Christian communities of love and accountability were also propelled into the world with a mission of witness and service. This is the origin of the evangelical egalitarian impulse of the Wesleyan Revival. All were equal in their condition of sin, but most important, all were equal in having been found by the searching grace of God in Jesus Christ. In status they were one, and in their evangelical responsibilities they had various callings.

Our attention is drawn first to the itinerant lay preachers. This is not because they were first in the order of appearing. The formation of societies on the local level preceded the organization of lay itinerant preaching. Nevertheless, it is difficult to conceive of the spread of the revival without the itinerant preaching. These were those whom Wesley declared as having been "raised up to provoke the *ordinary* ones to jealousy." The *ordinary* ones were, as Wesley viewed the matter, the pastor-priests who "exercised the priestly office" focusing centrally upon the celebration of the sacraments. On the other hand, there were those whom God had called to preach and evangelize. This was the *extraordinary* ministry alongside the *ordinary* ministry. It was not Wesley's intention to pit these two forms of ministry over against each other. Ideally, they were complimentary. The Holy Spirit constituted both orders as ministers.

While Wesley's distinction between the *ordinary* and *extraordinary* ministries may lack solid biblical justification, the distinction served his purposes once it was obvious to him that he needed the corps of traveling preachers. He reasoned that all who have been claimed by the saving grace of Christ are joined in the evangelical task of witnessing, not to themselves, but to the God of grace who in Jesus Christ had graced humanity by setting persons free from bondage to their self-will (justification) and setting them on a trajectory toward a life freed from the power of sin (sanctification). By virtue of the sanctifying grace of Christ, all Christians have a vocation, a calling, to witness in word, deed, and presence to the "glad tidings of salvation" in whatever position they find themselves. He explicitly spelled out this vocation to the traveling preachers:

> . . . never be unemployed, never be triflingly employed. Converse sparingly and cautiously with women; particularly with young women in private. . . . Do not affect the gentleman. You have no more to do with this character than with that of a dancing master. A preacher of the Gospel is the Servant of all. Be ashamed of nothing but sin: not of fetching wood (if time permit), or drawing water; not of cleaning your own shoes, or your neighbours'. Be punctual. Do everything exactly at the time. And, in general, do not mend our rules, but keep them. You have nothing to do but to save souls. Therefore, spend and be spent in the work. Observe. It is not your business to preach so many times . . . But to save as many souls as you can. Therefore, you will need all the sense you have, and to have your wits about you.

There were in Wesley's day "gospel preachers" about whom Wesley had nothing but contempt. They possessed a verbal catalogue of theological "catch words" that they shouted out with frequency to the delight of their hearers. Accordingly, Wesley warned his preachers:

> The gospel preachers so-called corrupt their hearers; they vitiate their taste, so that they cannot relish sound doctrine; and spoil their appetite, so that they cannot turn it into nourishment; they, as it were, freed them with sweetmeats, till the genuine wine of the kingdom seems quite insipid to them. They give them cordial upon cordial, which make them all life and spirit for the present; but, meantime, their appetite is destroyed, so that they can neither retain nor digest the pure milk of the word.[10]

The dropout rate for first generation itinerant preachers was considerable. The lay preachers who departed did so for a variety of reasons. Some simply fell out with Wesley, chafing under his heavy hand. Some left for personal reasons of health or marriage. Others sought ordination in the Anglican Church. However, the Holy Spirit and Mr. Wesley managed to find others to fill the ranks of this essential revival ministry.

On the local level in the societies, various lay ministries sustained the revival. Among these the most notable were the class leader, the exhorter, and the local preacher. Grace Murray's report from Newcastle is instructive:

Mr. Wesley fixed me in that part of the work which he thought proper and when the House (the Newcastle Orphan House) was finished, I was appointed to be the Housekeeper. Soon also, the people were again divided into Bands, or small select Societies; women by themselves, and the men in like manner. I had full a hundred in Classes, whom I met in two separate meetings, and a Band for each day of the week. I likewise visited the Sick and Backsliders. . . . We had also several societies in the country, which I regularly visited; meeting the women in the day time, and in the evening the whole society. And oh, what pourings out of the Spirit have I seen at those times![11]

This two-track system of lay ministry was not without its tensions. From time to time and place to place there were turf wars, but the pragmatic Wesley had captured in structure a fundamental principle of evangelism to which we today need to give concerted attention. Evangelism is not a ministry of the few; particularly it is not a professionalized ministry. Evangelism is a ministry that belongs to the whole people of God.

On the American side of the Atlantic this vision of evangelism belonging to the whole people of God began to recede about 1830. When the circuit rider began to dismount and become a stationed pastor, the local lay ministry of outreach and nurture began to undergo striking changes. Increasingly, the stationed pastor had responsibilities, or was perceived to have had, which had formerly been carried by laypersons. Male Class Leaders and exhorters tended to become the trustees of the church property. Women became active leaders in the Ladies' Aid Society, whose chief responsibilities were to "look out after the parsonage." In other words, the lay ministry of outreach increasingly became a ministry of institutional maintenance. What is even more serious is that the goal of institutional maintenance overshadowed the church's original self-identity—that of being a local mission society.

The Wesleyan Revival had its own historical and cultural context. Its context was the eighteenth century—not the twenty-first century. It would be sheer romanticism to assume that we can replicate the revival, piece by piece, just as Wesley practiced it. However, the Wesleyan Revival can instruct the practice of evangelism in the twenty-first century. Though we are prone to seek "quick fixes," surely God requires more and better of us than this.

What emerged in the revival of extraordinary importance for the people called Methodists was a distinctive pattern of the practice of evangelism—a practice that is theologically grounded, experientially sensitive, and structurally congruent with both the theological message and experiential "heart religion."

In practice, the pattern proceeded from the proclamation of the "glad tidings" to incorporation into a social entity (class and society), which then began a life-long process of nurture. The theological undergirding of the practice is nothing less than the message that Wesley proclaimed from 1739 to 1792: prevenient, justifying, and sanctifying grace. This is truly a remarkable synthesis of evangelical theology, evangelical experience, revival praxis, and a structural support system. To miss this is to miss the heart of the Wesleyan Revival. To miss this is to miss the relevance of Wesley for his children in the twenty-first century.

The Wesleyan Evangelical Pattern

Theological	Prevenient Grace	Justifying Grace	Sanctifying Grace
Practice	Preaching	Incorporation	Nurture
Experiential	Diseased Will	Healing	Vocation
Structural	Preaching Service	Class	Class & Society

In 1787 (four years before his death) Wesley embarked upon one last journey around the circuit of his societies and chapels. The old man wanted to see how his children were fairing. When he had completed this arduous journey, he retreated to a little village in upper Oxfordshire to reflect on his observations. To be truthful, he was not happy. What he had long feared seemed to be obvious to the eye. He had feared that the time would come when his people had "the form but not the power of religion." Now he sensed his fears were being fulfilled. Economically, the Methodists had begun the "upward climb." Socially, they had gained a measure of respectability. Experientially, the dynamic of grace in their lives was yesteryear. In short, the fires of revival and renewal were beginning to cool.

Wesley penned a sermon in that little Oxfordshire village. His text was Isaiah 5:1-3:

> Now will I sing to my well beloved
> a song of my beloved
> touching his vineyard.
> My well beloved
> hath a vineyard in a very fruitful hill.
> And he fenced it,
> and gathered out the stones thereof,
> and planted it with the choicest vines,
> and built a tower in the midst of it,
> and also made a wine press therein:
> and he looked that it should
> bring forth wild grapes.
> What could have been done
> to my vineyard,
> that I have not done in it?
> Wherefore, when I looked
> that it should bring forth grapes,
> brought it forth wild grapes?

Wesley had no inhibitions about appropriating the words of the Lord and placing them in his own mouth if the occasion demanded it. This was such an occasion. And so it is today.

"What could have been done to my vineyard, that I have not done?"

Discussion Questions

1. What three major practices enabled the Wesleyan Revival to outlast other revivals of the times?

2. "Practical divinity" involves mapping the places where divine grace intersects your life. If asked to create a road map of your spiritual life, what would you include?

3. In what ways was the class meeting an essential element of evangelism? What effect did the demise of the class meeting have on American Methodism?

4. When circuit riders became "stationed pastors" how were the ministries of the laity affected?

5. Discuss Wesley's expectation of the preaching moment. How does contemporary preaching align with Wesley's expectations?

Notes

1. Ronald A. Knox, *Enthusiasm* (Oxford: Oxford University Press, 1950), 475.

2. W. B. Fitzgerald, *The Roots of Methodism* (London: Charles H. Kelly, 1903), 173.

3. Charles Wesley, *Hymns for the Nativity of Our Lord* (Madison, NJ: The Charles Wesley Society, facsimile reprint of first edition, 1745).

4. Wesley, Sermon 85, "On Working Out Our Own Salvation," *Works,* 3:207.

5. Cf. *Journal* (March 13 1743). *Letters* (Telford) 6:36; and Letter to Joseph Benson (4 March 1774), *Letters* (Telforde) 6:77.

6. Albert Outler, *Evangelism in the Wesleyan Tradition* (Nashville: Tidings, 1971), 75.

7. *Journal,* April 5, 1739, in *Works* 19:47.

8. *Journal,* Jan. 11, 1744, in *Works* 20:7.

9. *Journal,* Jan. 25, 1744, in *Works 20:34.*

10. "Letter on Preaching," *Works* (Jackson), 11:489.

11. William Bennet, *Memoirs of Mrs. Grace Bennet* (Macclesfield: E. Bayley, 1803), 29.

CHAPTER THREE

Kindled by a Spark of Grace

The New Room in Bristol was packed to the doors with those who had come to hear the Rev. John Wesley preach. The expectant crowd represented a cross-section of the city. Men, women, and children of all ages, shopkeepers, aristocrats, craftsmen, coal miners, seamen and slaves were there. They had come from their mansions in Ratcliffe, their cottages in Stapleton, and their hovels in Kingswood to hear him preach. And preach he did. But before the message began the assembled crowd sang one of the hymns of the revival. They didn't need songbooks. The words were indelibly imprinted upon their memories. Verse after verse the momentum built until with a mighty crescendo they sang:

> Plenteous grace with thee is found,
>   Grace to cover all my sin;
> Let the healing streams abound,
>   Make and keep me pure within.
> Thou of life the fountain art,
>   Freely let me take of thee;
> Spring thou up within my heart;
>   Rise to all eternity.

Even before the delivery of the message, the chief note of the revival had been struck: "plenteous grace with thee is found."

Preaching, structures such as societies and classes, and a dynamic ministry of the laity were not the primary causes of the revival. They were what Wesley called the divinely-given "means of grace." Never should "means" be confused with "cause." John and Charles knew that a revival could not be humanly manufactured, though there was no revival without human agency. And while they were convinced that no revival occurs without the "means of grace," still only "a spark of grace" can be *the* cause. John rang the changes on this word "grace." "Universal grace." "Grace abounding." "Grace free for all and free in all." "Salvation by grace through faith." Salvation is the work of God. Salvation is a gracious gift of God, and it must not be confused with human achievement, with the exercise of the human will, or even with the faithful pursuit of a Christian lifestyle.

While Wesley vehemently at times opposed the Calvinist doctrine of election as a mistaken interpretation of the Pauline principle of "by grace alone," he insisted as much as Calvin that salvation is by divine grace and grace alone. He was convinced, however, that while God and God alone saves, God will not save us without ourselves.[1]

The human response to saving grace was important, but even the decision to accept God's grace was dependent upon the prior working of grace in the life of the believer. As Randy Maddox has stated, even " . . . the earliest inclination and ability to respond to God's saving action is dependent upon a renewing work of God's grace, without rendering our participation in this process automatic."[2] In short, God's initial work of grace is *prevenient*. It was Wesley's genius to see that the life of the Christian begins in grace and ends in grace—from grace to grace, grace upon grace. For Wesley's people, no phrase in their language was more important than "the grace of the Lord Jesus Christ."

The Meaning of Grace

Unlike most of us moderns, Wesley was a master of precision in his use of the English language. He spoke forthrightly what he meant, and he spoke with clarity and precision. By grace he meant what the New Testament plainly teaches: grace is neither God's general favor, nor God's mercy to our failure, nor God's pity for our pain. Grace is God's pardon and redemption in the face of our sin. Grace has its objective, and the objective is to restore a broken, sin-sick humanity to God and to one another.

Grace, then, is not God's act to improve humankind, but specifically grace is God's act to make new, to redeem.

Profound metaphysical truth can at times be found in the Mother Goose rhymes. For example:

Humpty Dumpty sat on a wall.
Humpty Dumpty had a great fall.
All the King's horses and all the King's men
Couldn't put Humpty Dumpty together again.

Only a work of grace can restore a Humpty Dumpty world!

Such a restoration has occurred and this Wesley knew as the gospel story —the *euangelion,* the *"good tidings."* The story begins even before Bethlehem. In the Hebrew Scriptures we read of God's showing forth God's *chesed,* variously rendered in our English versions as "mercy," "lovingkindness," "steadfast love." The Hebrew Scriptures speak of God as gracious towards helpless humanity and often at the same time declares that God is merciful, full of compassion, slow to anger, plenteous in mercy, and promises that God will abundantly pardon. Now in a Bethlehem night, in a Galilean ministry, culminating in a Jerusalem crucifixion and resurrection, the divine grace becomes a person in Jesus of Nazareth.

In the incarnate life and atoning death of Jesus Christ we find the stupendous expression of God's grace, freely given with no prerequisites. Stupendous indeed is God's act in Jesus Christ! One might expect some favor to be bestowed by a superior to a subordinate, the way a boss bestows a bonus to a faithful and hardworking employee. In the common vernacular we say that such is a "gracious act." But given the human condition of sin, alienation, and ungodliness, the act in Christ is not a common "gracious act." Jesus Christ is God's great "Nevertheless!" "God so loved the world that he gave his only Son . . . not to condemn the world, but that the world might be saved through him" (John 3:16). Let us know look at four attributes of grace.

Grace is, first, the very nature of God. In the older systematic theologies of what the Germans call *dogmatics*, grace was treated as an attribute of God. Grace was, so-to-speak, an adjective. In our time Karl Barth has taught us, among others, to correct this grammar. Freedom and loving are the very nature of God.

The Wesleys knew this also. They sang, "Pure, universal love Thou art." Out of the depths of divine freedom (Wesley's word was "sovereignty"), God acted. There was not external compulsion placed upon God. Grace is free in that it is unmerited. In his sermon, "The Witness of Our Spirits," Wesley stated clearly that the grace of God is " . . . that free love, that unmerited mercy, by which I, a sinner, through the merits of Christ am now reconciled to God."[3] On another occasion Wesley described grace in his *Instructions for Children* simply as " . . . the power of the Holy Ghost which enables us to believe and love and serve God."[4] And if God is "sovereign love," the inescapable conclusion is that God's grace is universal.

"For there is no distinction between Jew and Greek; for the same Lord is Lord of all . . . Whosoever shall call upon the name of the Lord shall be saved" (Romans 10:12-13). God has " . . . shut up all (men) unto disobedience, that he might have mercy upon all" (Romans 11:32), so that God's grace in Christ transcends all divisions of race, class, culture, creed or gender (Galatians 3:28; Colossians 3:11), " . . . for there is no respect of persons with God" (Romans 2:11). God's sovereignty lies in God's loving. Such love is indeed vulnerable. But only a God who is sovereignly free can choose to be vulnerable. Charles could treat this only by resorting to paradox:

> O Love divine, what hast thou done!
>   The immortal God hath died for me!
> The Father's co-eternal Son
>   Bore all my sins upon the tree!
> The immortal God for me hath died:
>   My Lord, my Love, is crucified.
>
> Is crucified for me and you,
>   To bring us rebels near to God;
> Believe, believe the record true,
>   Ye all are bought with Jesus' blood;
> Pardon for all flows from his side;
>   My Lord, my Love is crucified.

> Behold him, all ye that pass by,
>   The bleeding Prince of life and peace!
> Come, sinners, see your Saviour die,
>   And say, was ever grief like his?
> Come, feel with me his blood applied:
>   My Lord, my Love is crucified.[5]

Second, grace means quite simply "gift" (*charisma* in the singular, *charismata* in the plural). A gift cannot be earned; it can only be received. Grace is no mere kindly benevolence that is at everyone's beck and call. It is sheer gift. God gifts us not according to what we deserve but according to God's own love. God is love (1 John 4:8, 16), and God's love for us does not depend on what we are but on who God is! If the gift-character of God's relationship with us boggles our minds, then we are in good company. Hear Charles' question:

> Where shall my wondering soul begin?
> That I a child of wrath and hell—
> I should be called a child of God.

Third, grace is a Person. Grace has a name. The name is Jesus. Joseph had it on no greater authority than an angel of the Lord, " . . . you are to name him Jesus, for he will save his people from their sins" (Matthew 1:21). That God has dealt graciously in the past is a matter of biblical record, but here is something new. "And the Word became flesh and lived among us, and we have seen his glory, the glory as of a father's only son, full of grace and truth . . . From his fullness we have all received, grace upon grace" (John 1:14,16).

> Veiled in flesh the Godhead see!
>   Hail, the incarnate Deity!
> Pleased as man with men to dwell!
>   Jesus our Immanuel.

Fourth, the work of grace effects a restoration or a new relationship with God and with our neighbor. On occasion Wesley would speak of the restoration of the divine image in us as the uncompromising love for God and neighbor—the fulfillment of the law and the prophets. To those who receive it, the grace of God means first and foremost the forgiveness of sins and a new standing with God (justification). They enter into a new relationship with God that is determined solely by divine grace, and in which they can be described as being in a *state of grace*. This same grace then becomes a power in their lives, producing a new outlook, attitude, spirit, and temper like God's own (sanctification).

> Jesus, confirm my heart's desire
>   To work, and speak and think for thee;
> Still let me guard the holy fire
>   And still stir up thy gift in me.

Not only does Wesley offer us an unambiguous definition of grace, he also exhibits a remarkable logic that is inherent within grace itself. By logic I mean something like grammar. Grammatically, a complete sentence demands a *subject*, an *object*, a *verb* and a *period*. Otherwise the syntax does not pass the test of being "good" grammar or "good" logic.

Wesley's message was that always and without qualification the God of grace is the *subject* of the sentence. Herein lies the human dilemma. The problem with Adam and Eve and with all modern Adams and Eves is that we want to make ourselves the *subject* of the sentence. The heart of human sin is that humans want to jump over the verb and become the subject of the sentence. In grace, however, God always takes the initiative. It is not we who find God, but God in Christ finds us. You may recall the old bumper stickers of several decades ago, "I've found it!" In spite of all the good intentions, this was not good Christian grammar. Good Christian grammar says, "I have been found" or the grace of Christ has found me.

A broken, gnarled, twisted, distorted, sinful humanity is the *object* in the sentence of grace. If grace is *gift,* then we are the recipients of that unmerited divine gratuity.

While Wesley never ceased to praise the God of grace, and while his eye never ceased to focus upon a fallen humankind, his message was preeminently of the *verb.* The God of grace in Jesus Christ has acted to restore or redeem. The human fault lies in a diseased will, and only that which comes to us from without can restore, redeem, or heal.

Without grace the human will can only will itself. The full work of grace in healing or restoring the will

Wesley saw as threefold: prevenient, justifying and sanctifying.

The grace of Christ "goes before" us ("pre-vents" to use Wesley's term). This "going before" action is present in some measure in all persons. This is the action that awakens a slumbering humanity and opens closed eyes, so that humans may behold their condition before God. Awakened, we are able to see the law of God for what it is, and consequently see ourselves for who we are. We are those who make a law unto ourselves. We are the ones who are always trying to leap over the *verb* and become the *subject*. We are the ones not content to be creatures but who continually attempt to usurp the role of creator. The simple word that describes this condition is sin.

If we are sensitive to this "going before" action of God, we will know in the depths of our beings something of St. Paul's poignant cry, "Wretched man that I am! Who will deliver me from this death?" (Romans 7:24). We are sunk in Godly despair. Knowing that we cannot heal ourselves, we can only repent, but without the "going before" action of Christ, we would not have the power to repent. Repentance is not, therefore, a work of the law. Astoundingly, it is a work of grace! It is God who gives us the power to repent. But this is not the end of the *sentence*. It is also God who makes *faith* possible when we hear the *verb*.

The *verb* is *justify*, or, as Wesley put it, *pardon*. The God of grace in Christ not only goes before us. The God of grace in Christ meets us where we are in our wilderness experience. God in Christ speaks the word of forgiveness. This word of pardon, Wesley proclaimed, is God's liberating act, setting us free from the bondage to self-will or guilt. The late Paul Tillich and others have claimed that modern people do not experience guilt in the way in which Victorians did. What these theologians seemingly cannot do is explain why our age has become the most self-justifying age in history. Compulsively, we engage in all kinds of patterns of self-justification hoping to make ourselves acceptable, if not to God, then to ourselves. The Christian claim that only Christ can justify sets the believer free from these subtle, compulsive patterns of self-justification. And subtle they are! Wesley's friend, a former slave ship seaman turned evangelical Anglican cleric, John Newton put it this way:

> 'Twas grace that taught my heart to fear,
>   And grace my fears relieved;
> How precious did that grace appear
>   The hour I first believed.

For Wesley, there was another important *verb* in the sentence of grace. God through the Holy Spirit *sanctifies*. "Inward and outward holiness" was Wesley's way of expressing it. "Without holiness no person shall see God" (Hebrews 12:14), was Wesley's frequent admonition. The word "holy" when used of the characteristics of God, such as "holy love," is an adjective of adjectives and pertains to the infinitely perfect characteristics of God, and to the fact that all God's characteristics are in a relationship of harmony with each other. God is not at odds with God's self.

When we are called to be holy we are called to live in a relationship of integrity and harmony with the will and character of God. It is a call to flesh out the family likeness of God's family. "As obedient children, do not be conformed to the passions of your former ignorance, but as he who called you is holy, be holy yourselves in all your conduct . . . " (1 Peter 1:14-15).

In our so-called post-modern society, different voices can be heard today appealing in various ways for Christians to stand up and demonstrate, out of faith conviction and evangelical experience, the dissonance emitted when a genuinely grace-formed life comes up against the dominant culture or cultures. In many ways the truly grace-filled life is counterculture to the marketplace. The logic of the marketplace is the logic of exchange. It is the logic of acquisition, getting, and achieving. The logic of getting ushers in a lifestyle of calculation. On the other hand, the logic of grace is the logic of receiving, which ushers in a lifestyle of giving and sharing.

One voice calls Christians to become a "cognitive deviant minority." Others speak of a Christian, countercultural expression of the Sermon on the Mount. And another calls for a "third race" composed of revolutionary Christians who set themselves against the cultural tides, representing the new creation, the joyous people of the kingdom of God.

All of these have truth in them, but one thing is missing, Wesley would insist. We do not make ourselves holy. We seek that sanctified life which only God in Christ through the Holy Spirit can give. To be sure, we are not made holy independently of ourselves. It is the presence and power of the Holy Spirit that enables us to enter into the co-operant relationship with God, whereby our lives do become different, new, renewed in the divine image. Talk about holiness can often degenerate into a moralistic legalism, or into a theological abstraction. True holiness is neither.

That which caused Wesley more difficulty in his time than any other single article of faith was entire sanctification, or perfection. This was at the heart of the Calvinist-Wesleyan controversy in his time. Across the centuries the doctrine of entire sanctification or holiness has been controversial for Wesley's children, whether these controversies were challenges from without or conflicts from within. This has been so much the case that many Methodists no longer even speak the language of perfection. But to use the logic of grammar, perfection in love, singleness of motive, is in a real sense the *period* of the sentence of grace. In other words, in Wesleyan logic the sentence of grace is not complete without the *period*. What goes before in terms of prevenient, justifying, and sanctifying grace doesn't quite make logical sense without recognizing that perfection in love is God's ultimate purpose for all God's people.

Confusion remains among both Methodists and non-Methodists concerning the doctrine of perfection, so it is important to carefully define it. Wesley's understanding of perfection did not include an argument for a sinless perfection. When speaking of entire sanctification or perfection, Wesley was pointing to the possibility that the Holy Spirit could purify our varying and conflicting motives to the point where we will, or act, with a single motive: the God-given motive of love for God and for the neighbor. In this sense perfection in love is God's ultimate purpose. And mind you, God always completes the sentence!

As Christians, we are called to express our faith in the one, full, complete sentence of grace, including the *period*. The late Bishop Nolan Harman, when reading the historic Wesleyan question to ordinands, would always pause when he came to the question, "Are you going on to perfection?" Then he would add his own question, "If you are not going on to perfection, then tell me where are you going?"

You will notice that I have said nothing yet about the Wesleyan emphasis on the New Birth or regeneration. Yet, this article is what makes the Wesleyan position on grace truly evangelical. The New Birth does not interrupt the grammatical flow of the sentence. In fact, it is the internal logic of the whole sentence.

New Birth is what holds justification and sanctification in an inseparable relationship. Without the New Birth, justification becomes what Dietrich Bonhoeffer called "cheap grace," and what Wesley called Antinomianism.[6] Without the New Birth, sanctification becomes another form of works' righteousness or seeking one's salvation by "good works."

Wesley's understanding of the New Birth was considerably richer than our inheritance from nineteenth century revivalism. In nineteenth century revivalism New Birth became so psychologized that it almost lost all its content of meaning. Being "born again" came more to be a terminal point in the life of the Christian rather than a beginning point. Not so for Wesley. For Wesley, at the moment of our justification we are given the "power of a new affection," namely, Christ shares the divine love with us. At that same moment the Holy Spirit acts, in Wesley's words, to implant the "seeds of the holy tempers" in our being. That word "temper" is now archaic, but we could just as easily translate it as "virtue." The Holy Spirit plants within the soil of the new love or affection these seeds of virtue that, if properly cared for and cultivated, will grow into the "fruits of the Spirit." For Wesley, there were only two indicators of the New Birth: the inward witness of the Spirit and the outward manifestation of the "fruits of the Spirit." It is not possible for one to be without the other.

And so the sentence is completed. One whole, coherent, logical sentence with God the *subject*, we humans the *object* and the work of Christ through the Holy Spirit the *verb*, to the end that a lost people are found, a sin-diseased people are healed, and God's new creation is finished, "lost in wonder, love, and praise." The sentence of grace is a mighty sentence and the bedrock of a Wesleyan evangelism.

Methodists have not always lived comfortably with this Wesleyan vision of grace. As a community of forgiven sinners, we constantly try to bring this gospel under our control. We do this by reducing the gospel to manageable proportions. Reductionism is the greatest sin of the Church! We don't have to take the Jesus Seminar as a prime example. Instead, we may look at ourselves. We have reduced church membership to a ritual comparable to the process of joining a social club, and the social club has higher expectations of its members. We have practiced reductionism regarding infant baptism' reducing the sacrament to a parental dedication service, or indiscriminately celebrating the sacrament without regard for church discipline. And we have done it with our Christology, our faith in Christ. The late New York columnist, Dorothy Parker, once remarked that most American Protestants felt about Jesus the way she felt about her maid. They could give him a good recommendation any day! And sadly, the list of reductionisms could be lengthened.

No doubt the greatest reductionism is what we have done with salvation itself. I confess that there was something I overlooked when I first read Karl Barth's

Church Dogmatics. In recent years I have come to reclaim it. In his *Church Dogmatics,* IV, 3/2, by historical analysis Barth showed convincingly that whereas the biblical understanding of salvation is both divine forgiveness and divine calling to witness, or in Wesleyan terms, justification and sanctification, we have reduced the meaning of salvation almost to the point of an "impious egocentricity." My discovery has come, not so much by struggling with Barth, but by grappling with the richness of Wesley's repeated insistence on the inseparability of justification and sanctification.[7]

We are the inheritors of a tradition from the nineteenth century that has separated the two, benefit and calling, justification and sanctification. In the case of salvation, we have reduced the meaning to an almost exclusive concentration on personal benefit, to the neglect of calling to sanctification or discipleship.

We must emphasize the personal and individual expressions of faith. The human side of the experience of faith, however, can become too human, as though the entire purpose of the suffering of Christ were a person's "cozy happiness." If we had held together the divine benefit of forgiveness with the divine calling to witness, would we have to indulge in frantic efforts to get believers to witness to their faith when we suddenly discover that the numbers on our membership rolls are drastically sagging? My appeal is not that we must necessarily use Wesley's words, but to miss his logic is to compromise the wholeness of the Gospel.

Such a robust view of grace or salvation demands a mighty Christ. For Wesley, to compromise our witness to Christ is to compromise salvation itself. Wesley writes:

> It is our part thus to "preach Christ" by preaching all things whatsoever he hath revealed. We may indeed, without blame, yea, and with a peculiar blessing from God, declare the love of our Lord Jesus Christ; . . . But still we should not "preach Christ" according to His word if we are wholly to confine ourselves to this. We are not ourselves clear before God unless proclaim him all his offices. To preach Christ as a workman that needeth not to be ashamed is to preach him not only as our great "High Priest" . . . but likewise as the Prophet of the Lord, "who of God is made unto us wisdom," who by his Word and his Spirit "is with us always," "guiding us into all truth"; yea, and as a remaining a King for ever; as giving laws to all whom He has bought with his blood; as restoring those to the image of God whom he had first reinstated in his favour; as reigning in all believing hearts until he has "subdued all things to Himself"; until He hath utterly cast out all sin, and "brought in everlasting righteousness."[8]

Wesley's Christ was Lord as well as Savior, Prophet as well as Priest. Thus for Wesley, as Albert Outler stated thirty-two years ago, "evangelism was more than conversion and regeneration. It was instead both initiation and maturation in Christ and in Christian fellowship, and an implicit, indirect social revolution."[9]

While Wesley's message was the message of grace, one could also say that it was the expression of a rediscovered Christology (of all things, from John Calvin!). "Preach Christ in his fullness," Wesley constantly admonished his helpers. That is to say, "Preach Christ as Prophet, Priest, and King." The canonical narrative of scripture is summed in that Christology, and the grace of Christ is the hermeneutical key to it all. The prevenient grace of Christ the Prophet reveals the law that convicts us. The justifying grace of Christ the Priest sets us in a new relationship with God. And the sanctifying grace of Christ the King places us under the Lordship of Christ.

Such a high view of Christ requires, likewise, a high view of God. A Wesleyan cannot avoid confessing faith in the triune God. The Wesleyan understanding of grace entails a confession of faith in Christ who is the revelation of the triune God: Father, Son, and Spirit. Belief in the triune God is not only a logical presupposition to Wesley's Christology; our belief in the triune God is fraught with evangelistic implications. The Trinitarian interaction between Father, Son, and Spirit in the early centuries was spoken of as "sending" or "mission." The Trinitarian action of the Father sending the Son and the Father and the Son sending the Spirit form the ground of the evangelical imperative and its authority. In other words, the evangelical imperative is rooted in the very being of the sending God, made manifest in the life, death, and resurrection of Jesus Christ through the Holy Spirit.[10] This is not abstract speculation. Hear St. Paul's words:

> But when the fullness of time was come, God sent forth his Son . . . to redeem them that were under the law, that we might receive the adoption of sons. And because you are sons, God has sent forth the Spirit of his Son into your hearts, crying, "Abba, Father."[11]

Our God is a "sending" God, and we, in turn, are a "sent" people. We are certainly motivated to witness by the need that we see in people around us. Human need is a powerful motive. But the question remains, "Why are we motivated by human need?" It is because the priority of God is to reach out to the least, the last, and the lost. And as God has sent the Son and the Spirit, so through the Son and the Spirit we are sent. The authority, motive, and goal of evangelism are implicit in the sentence of grace itself.[12] And so the Wesleyans sang:

> O that the world might taste and see
>   The riches of his grace!
> The arms of love the compass me
>   Would all the world embrace.

Discussion Questions

1. What was Wesley's understanding of the definition and objective of grace as taught in the New Testament?

2. What was Wesley's definition of Christian perfection? In what ways is God currently assisting you in your journey toward Christian perfection?

3. For Wesley, the New Birth or justification marked a new beginning. What new things occur in a person's life at the New Birth and what two things indicate that the New Birth has occurred?

NOTES

1. See James C. Logan, "Free Grace: Wesley's Theology and the Calvinist Challenge," in *Virginia United Methodist Heritage,* XXIX, 2, Fall 2003, pp.21-31.

2. Randy Maddox, *Responsible Grace: John Wesley's Practical Theology* (Nashville: Kingswood Books, 1994), 64.

3. Sermon 12, "The Witness of Our Own Spirit," *Works,* I:309.

4. Wesley, *Instructions for Children* (Bristol: William Pine, 1767, eighth edition).

5. *A Collection of Hymns for the Use of the People Called Methodists,* in Works, 7:114.

6. Literally antinomianism (from *anti*, against, and *nomos*, law) claims that Christians are not bound by moral law. While there has never been a party in the Church called "antinomian," Wesley was convinced that the Calvinist logic of "once saved, always saved" led inevitably to moral indifference, hence a neglect of the life of holiness or sanctification.

7. Darrell Guder in his recent book, *The Continuing Conversion of the Church* (Grand Rapids, MI: W. B. Eerdmans, 2000) draws attention to the same Barthian references.

8. Sermon, "The Law Established through Faith, II," *Works* 2:37-38.

9. Albert Outler, *Evangelism in the Wesleyan Spirit* (Nashville: Tidings, 1974).

10. Note the "sending" language in the Nicene Creed.

11. Galatians 4:4-6a, RSV.

12. For a hymnic treatment of the Trinitarian basis of the evangelical imperative, see Charles Wesley's hymn, "Come Father, Son and Holy Ghost," in *Works* 7:646-47 (No. 464). Also, for a fuller commentary on the Trinitarian base of the evangelical imperative, see James C. Logan. "The Evangelical Imperative: A Wesleyan Perspective," in Logan, ed., *Theology and Evangelism in the Wesleyan Heritage* (Nashville: Kingswood Books, 1994), 15-33.

CHAPTER FOUR

O That All Might Catch the Flame

Given our concerns for a recovery of evangelistic commitment and zeal in our churches, we could easily, but mistakenly, conclude that all we need to do is repeat Wesley in word and structure, subscribing to a kind of Wesleyan literalism. Wesley's world was eighteenth century England. Wesley's church was an establishment church. Even though Wesley had some unkind remarks to make about a Constantinian Church, in a very real sense such was the Anglican Church of his day. For example, in his day one's only credential for citizenship in the body politic was the entry of one's name on the baptismal registry in the parish church.

Eighteenth century English society was in ferment. The Industrial Revolution was just beginning, accompanied with massive population relocation from impoverished rural areas to equally impoverished urban centers. These demographic shifts put great stress upon the established order of the Anglican parish. Structurally, the state church was not equipped to deal with the population mobility. While we experience today population mobility, our demographic picture is greatly different from the picture of Wesley's eighteenth century. Our population shifts are global, rather than local and regional.

Politically, the rise of the democratic spirit literally frightened Wesley out of his wits. And yet, across the Atlantic the great democratic experiment was actually taking place. Our political context today is not the eighteenth century shift from agrarian to industrial society, from monarchy to democracy, and from the remnants of an economic feudal order to a new capitalistic order.

Intellectually, Wesley's century reveled and flourished in the Enlightenment mentality. John Locke's epistemology offered the foundations of a thoroughgoing empiricism. High confidence in the development and fruits of the physical sciences shaped the mind of the intelligentsia. Wesley, to a limited extent, agreed with Locke's empiricism. The high regard for reason and rational discourse marked the day, and Wesley, esteemed the role of reason as well. Yet, Wesley was not fully and without reserve an Enlightenment man. At the same time, the intellectual context within which he ministered was

Enlightenment, explicitly for the educated and cultured of the society, and Enlightenment sentiments trickled down to the common folk. Today, the Enlightenment mentality is being questioned in many quarters of our society. Some say that we are entering a post-Enlightenment or post-modern era, whatever "post" may mean, and its meaning varies from one observer to another. Nevertheless, whatever label is put on the times, our times are markedly different from Wesley's times.

Has Wesley anything to say to us as we enter the twenty-first century? Ours is not the Industrial Revolution, but the advanced stages of the technological revolution. Our church is not the state church of Anglicanism. In our time the global scene becomes localized in our living rooms as we watch television, or along the streets where we hear the different languages at our doorsteps. The generations from boomers on have learned to perceive not so much through the printed word as through the virtual word. The list of differences could be extended.

It would be anachronistic and downright unfair to Wesley to attempt to make him a "quick-fix" for all that ails us. On a deeper level than offering Wesleyan band-aids, there is a way to find profound significance of Wesley and the Wesleyan Revival for us today. The Wesleyan Revival was consumed with a vision—a grand vision of the grace of God in Jesus Christ, working through the means of the Holy Spirit. Consider again the diagram of the

Wesleyan synthesis in the preceding chapter that presents a holistic and integrated vision of revival.

Much of contemporary evangelism focuses on technique and method, but technique and method without a vision. Precisely at this point Wesley can speak to us where we most need his aid. Wesley developed his methods and techniques, but they were always critiqued and normalized by the vision. They did not create the vision, but instead served the vision. If we endeavor to listen to Wesley, we will listen with sharply critical, analytical sensitivity, for ours is a new era. The contemporary church finds itself in a new cultural location unlike any possible parallel, unless we find it in the New Testament church in *The Acts of the Apostles*. Maybe, perchance, Wesley can speak to us, clearing our confused minds, riding us of bad habits of thought and practice, and giving us a new vision. It's worth the try.

Post-Christendom: A New Situation

If we were to drive down the Autostrada from Milan to Rome, we could in our imaginations journey back to Christendom. On either side of the highway we view the Umbrian hills with those medieval towns situated atop the hills, complete with city walls. We notice from the highway the spire of the village, town, or city church, piercing the skyline. Turning off the highway and following the meandering road up the hillside to the city walls, finding the gate in the wall, and entering into the town, we find an interesting example of ancient city planning. We discover that the church with the piercing spire that shot into the sky is actually at the very center of the town. The streets literally radiate out from the church square like spokes radiating out from the hub of a wheel. This is an expression of a time when the church was not only physically, but also literally, at the center of things. The church legitimated, and even at times originated, the values that governed the society. In fact, it was difficult to distinguish between civic life and church life. They were one unified society. In another sense, the church was the glue that held the society together. The church was the primary social, political, intellectual, as well as spiritual institution of the society. This was Christendom!

In this country, from the days of the formation of the Constitution, we have hallowed the principle of "separation of church and state." At the same we have informally had our own little Protestant Christendoms. I grew up in a county seat town in the South that was one of these little Christendoms. In former times no one worried about the future of the church. In the social order of things the church had a fixed position closely allied with the civil powers. We lived in a church establishment. The church enjoyed a privileged position in the society. The older established churches may have had their distinguishing differences, but they were more social than theological. The older aristocratic families belonged to the Episcopal and Presbyterian churches. The merchant class and professionals belonged to the Methodist church. The textile factory supervisors and small shop owners belonged to the Baptist church. And if you were of the "working poor" or just plain "poor poor" you belonged to one of the so-called "sect" churches over on the other side of the railroad tracks. In any event, you *belonged*. In fact, if you had no church identification, there surely was something wrong with your character. The church, whatever denomination, was a fixed institution. The church was established. We were a "churched" town. We were a little Christendom.

As the twenty-first century unfolds, the ground has shifted beneath the feet of church-going Americans. No longer is it a given that people will go to church, or even ever set foot inside a church. No longer are vast numbers of people eager to "join," certainly not to join a community with a message that includes words of self-denial and sacrifice. No longer is the church automatically considered an asset to the community. The society that once called itself Christian now has new values, new habits, new saints, new gods, and, so it assumes, new and better places to get its religion than the neighborhood church on the corner. Though once virtually everybody went to church, that day has been replaced by a more secular age when the mainline church seems increasingly on the sideline in a society that is less interested in and less hospitable to it. This is a post-Christendom! As Dorothy said to Toto, "I don't think we're in Kansas anymore."

I know that there is danger in universalizing one's own particular experience. At the same time others could create scenarios and narratives strikingly similar to the one I have drawn. Where the church once held a privileged, established position in the cultural mind, today this is increasingly not the case. A neighbor once remarked to me, "I know that we should go to church. But, you see, there are so many good causes today."

Where once we could consider the general culture to be at least nominally Christian, today the church finds itself in what Alfred Krass has called "a neo-pagan North America."[1] Where once we thought of mission as something done geographically over there and done by the church mostly by proxy, today even the local church finds itself literally in a missionary situation. During the period of the church's privileged, culturally established placement, we acquired some very bad habits regarding evangelism, and now we will have to do something that Wesley did not have to do. We will have to un-learn in order to re-learn what authentic, vital evangelism is. I list only a few of these bad habits; you could extend the list:

Bad Habit #1

We became convinced that evangelism is something done by clergy and other trained professionals. Frequently a few members took on the thankless task of "doing evangelism" on behalf of the rest. And the gospel failed to be told as it should have been because members were reluctant to open their lips.

Bad Habit #2

We came to think of evangelism as membership recruitment or the quantitative increase in church membership. Hence, we looked to the Sunday schools and confirmation classes to find our new "recruits," and we failed to reach out to the so-called "un-reached." We failed to see that many times, while Sunday school may have produced church members, it did not necessarily produce Christians! Even when we reached outside the church, we sought others who were already church members, and so transfer of membership became a component of evangelism.

Bad Habit #3

We became so institutionally comfortable that we claimed that the church is here on this corner, our doors are open, and we will gladly welcome anyone who comes. This is what I call "fly paper" evangelism! Several things were wrong with this stance. One, our "welcoming spirit" tended to confine our own kind socially, economically, and racially. Two, we received persons into our membership on the basis of the lowest possible common denominator in terms of discipleship. And it is no mystery why we have a body of people within most of our congregations who know just enough about the Christian faith to be immunized from the real thing. In effect, what we were doing, and calling it evangelism, was supplying "ecclesiastical housing" for "cultural Christians."

Bad Habit #4

We became convinced that proactive, penetrative evangelism into our neighborhoods, communities, cities, and countrysides was not culturally and socially acceptable behavior. We left such behavior to the Salvation Army and then placated our consciences by dropping a dollar into the kettle at the ring of a bell at Christmastime.

Bad Habit #5

In many of our congregations evangelism became reduced to a matter of "saving" individual persons from the world, rather than leading them to a conversion to a whole new world of discipleship to Jesus Christ lived out as righteousness, justice, and love. The late E. Stanley Jones once remarked, "Evangelism without social action is like a soul without a body. One is a ghost and the other is a corpse. We don't want either. We must keep evangelism and social action together. Then we have a living organism." Jones's observation illustrates classic Wesleyanism in a more modern vernacular.

Bad Habit #6

By the 1950s the local congregation appeared to lack the intrinsic vitality of grace that had once birthed and sustained a people whose self-identity was innately missional. The congregation had become more and more concerned about maintaining its position, status, and structure within what was assumed to be the established order. The congregation then looked to the superstructure of the church (episcopacy, boards, and agencies) for the programmatic impetus for missional engagement, as though to say, "Give us banners. We can march better under banners!" The congregation looked to the superstructure for missional priorities, drives, emphases, and new programs as though these were "vitamin shots" that would restore the missional vitality lost from the body. Lacking in intrinsic motivation we sought the remedy in extrinsic motivation. We had forgotten the lesson (or did we ever learn it?) from childhood. The appeal to extrinsic motivation as Christmas neared, "Be good for Santa is coming," probably never lasted longer than twenty-four hours, to say nothing about the dubious method of moral formation by promises and rewards!

The list of bad habits could continue, but what is more urgent is to probe behind these habits to grasp the picture of what was happening. In truth, the congregation's own self-understanding had been shifting from a missional self-understanding to an inwardly directed, institutional self-understanding. This was because the North American context accepted and promoted the legitimacy of the Christian enterprise. Congregations and connectional denominations did not have to wrestle with their core identity over against a hostile or indifferent world. Church and world were joined in a common enterprise. The church did not have to make distinct its identity vis-à-vis the dominant culture. It plainly had incarnated that culture.

We did not begin to awaken to this dilemma until, in recent decades, we were confronted with an increasingly diverse culture, stagnation and decline in our membership, loss of privileged prestige, rise of uneasiness, and downright distrust of denominational regulatory power. All of these are indicators of what Kennon Callahan calls "the erosion of a churched culture."[2]

If this brief analysis is correct, the contemporary church finds itself in the posture of trying to maintain the vestiges of a collapsing paradigm rather than imaging itself as an apostolic, missionary people. What would be required for the church to move from a maintenance mentality to a genuinely committed new, yet ancient, understanding of being a missionary people?

First, an exorcism of the inherited bad habits will be necessary. After spending the last ten years concentrating almost exclusively on evangelism in a seminary curriculum, I have come to the conviction that we must experience a purgation of these bad habits—and they are entrenched—which we carry as a dubious inheritance from a Christendom church. The problem is deep within the life of our local congregations. We, as the local church, look to the very boards and agencies (which we at the same time distrust) and fail to realize that the "log is in our own eye." Where is the passion for Jesus Christ in our local congregations? Is our failure to name the name of Jesus in the public marketplace due to a demotion in rank of him in our own lives and the life of our congregations? If the basic problem is in the congregation, why should we look elsewhere for the solution?

Second, a faithful and effective ministry of evangelism depends upon a conversion of our congregations from maintenance to mission. Not just the pastor, not just a few members of an evangelism committee, but the congregation is the primary agent of the evangelical witness. The urgent task is to form new congregations or re-form existing congregations into people whose primary identity is to be Christ's "sent people." A faithful and effective ministry of evangelism today requires apostolic, missional congregations full of people who know this missional identity in the depths of their collective beings, and who live out that identity with responsible passion. The God of providential grace is able and ready to give us another possibility, a new form, indeed a new life. But we can accept this gift of the new only as we relinquish the old to which we so stubbornly cling. We will not be awakened to this new possibility as long as we are content to play the redundant role of a Christendom, official religious cult in our society.

Wesley's Vision Today

Wesley knew that the revival was not the result of his leadership along with a few select individuals. Evangelism requires a people, not a corps or a committee. The late Halford Luccock, a prophetic Methodist of another generation and taught preaching to hundreds of seminarians at Yale, told a story of being in a small midwestern town on a Saturday evening to begin a preaching mission the next day in the local Methodist church. He perused the weekly county newspaper, and was fascinated to read the account of the local PTA meeting. One item in the account particularly caught his attention. It read, "Last night at the PTA meeting Mabel Jones whistled Beethoven's Fifth Symphony." Luccock said that he had no doubt that Mabel Jones was a very fine person, but she couldn't possible whistle Beethoven's Fifth. It takes a full symphony orchestra for that. Evangelism is like that. It requires a full orchestra.

Wesley knew that. The evangelistic task could not be effectively pursued with only the itinerating preachers, as important as they were. Evangelism required a local congregation that understood God had called each and every person to some form of witness.

Evangelism required the local society, constituted as it was with the classes. Evangelism required the class leader, the exhorter, and the local preacher, along with the itinerating preachers. Speaking the "glad tidings" and supervising the discipline of the small group as members grew in sanctification were both crucial to the evangelistic task of reaching unreached persons. Even those who did not have the desired skills witnessed. S. T. Kimbrough points to a poem by Charles Wesley about Elizabeth Blackwell, wife of a noted London banker. She proclaimed God's Good News and never uttered a word. Others came to their faith in Christ through the power of the gospel she lived.

> By wisdom pure and peaceable,
>   By the meek Spirit of her Lord,
> She knows the stoutest to compel
>   And sinners wins without a word;
> They see the tempers of the Lamb,
>   And bow subdued to Jesus' name,
> As captives of resistless Love.[3]

Evangelism continues to suffer from compartmentalization. Until a congregation comes to sense its corporate identity as an evangelizing congregation, much of our evangelistic ministry will be stalemated.

Our conventional understanding of church actually gets in the way of effective evangelistic ministry. David Bosch, in that magisterial work, *Transforming Mission*, captures this well. "Church," Bosch said, is conceived in this view as *the place* where a Christianized civilization gathers for worship, and *the place* where the Christian character of the society is cultivated. Increasingly, this view of the church as a "place where certain things happen" located the church's self-identity in its organizational forms and its professional class, the clergy, who perform the church's authoritative activities. Popular grammar aptly illustrates: you "go to church" much the same way you might go to a store. You "attend" a church, the way you attend a school or theater. You "belong to a church" as you would a service club with its programs and activities. This is still the Christendom church. A Christendom church has "place." The very stance of having "place" gets in the way of missional outreach.[4]

In the Wesleyan Revival the local societies were not so much "places" as components in a larger, on-going missional "movement." One could even argue that as the societies established themselves, bought property, and called themselves chapels—all of which was acquiring "place"—they began to lose their evangelical zeal. More and more they took on the character of what Wesley had feared. " . . . having the form but not the power of religion."

To counter such an understanding of church, some leaders in evangelism have recently begun to speak of the church as an "apostolic" people. What a transformation would be actualized if our congregations knew themselves not as "kept" people but as "sent people." The early Wesleyans knew that their identity consisted in their calling, and that was to be a missionary movement.

The One Thing Required

John Wesley knew both by analysis and instinct that the culture of eighteenth century England (and even the culture of much of the Hanoverian Anglican Church) was not sufficient to carry the weight of creditability of the Christian gospel. Wesley knew that persons could not become Christians and grow as Christians without a supporting and legitimating culture.

This is what he meant when he remarked that there is no religion that is not social. I do not desire to minimize the Wesleyan social passion. I want to affirm that social passion and own it for myself and for my church. But in spite of modern attempts to make the statement "no religion which is not social" the capstone of his social convictions about wealth, the poor, and the institution of slavery, Wesley's intention was to underscore another point. We do not become Christians in isolation. We become Christians in community. We become Christians in a culture where the politics is not "power politics," but the politics of forgiveness. We become Christians in a culture where hospitable social behavior is not the "pat on the back," but where, regardless of race or economic "pecking order," Christians gather around a common table as forgiven sisters and brothers. This is a culture that grows not by biological propagation but by evangelism.[5]

For Wesley, if the broader culture, and even the culture of the church at that time, could not perform this task, then an alternative culture was desperately needed. It was for this reason Wesley formed and shaped the local societies and classes. Here was the culture where the message of grace could ring with a self-evident credibility. Here was the culture where persons could meet the crucified and risen Christ, could know their sins forgiven, could experience the presence and power of the Holy Spirit making them into new beings in Christ Jesus. Here was a culture that rejected the calculating logic of the market, and chose to live by the life-giving logic of grace. Wesley knew this to be absolutely essential to the task at hand of "spreading scriptural holiness over the land."

If this was essential to Wesley's mission, how much more so is it for the contemporary church? Peter Berger, some years ago, analyzed the breakdown in Western, and particularly American, culture in terms of what he called credibility structures. These had been the general social structures that, in another time, had carried the weight of credibility of Christian conviction.[6] When the "sacred canopy" of a so-called Christian culture collapses, the church that has depended upon these structures finds itself in a quandary. Does it bury it head in the sand in ostrich fashion and pretend that nothing has happened? Does it run in panic like Henny Penny crying, "The sky is coming down"? Good Wesleyans would do neither. Good Wesleyans would set themselves to the task of creating an alternative culture of grace.

A Culture of Grace

What would a culture of grace look like? What were Wesley's concerns in forming the societies or classes as an alternative culture? Wesley certainly did not reduce the Christian faith to a matter of private religiosity. Clearly, he saw the practice of Christian faith as "apostolic" — being a sent people. Yet, it is not adequate to define "apostolic" simply in terms of activity. What constitutes "being a sent people?" If a "sent people" are people of a distinctive faith community, what, then, are the dynamics of a community of "apostles?"

Richard Steele has edited an extraordinary collection of essays on Wesleyan "heart religion."[7] In his introduction to the essays he discerns that in the life of the individual Christian, Wesley saw the essence of Christian faith as consisting of a "cord of three strands," a dynamic complex of three distinct but inseparable and equally necessary ways by which a Christian stands related to the living God. These he enumerates as "right belief," "right conduct," and "right passion." I would add that what applies to the "apostle" (the one sent) applies equally to the "apostolic people" (a sent people).

Right Belief: Wesley was of a "catholic mind" (open to differing opinions), but he was not doctrinally indifferent. Doctrine mattered. At times he could disparage "mere orthodoxy," the cognitive consent to certain propositional doctrines. But he contrasted "mere orthodoxy" with "vital orthodoxy." In "vital orthodoxy" the same doctrines shaped and directed the formation of

Christian character. In other words, Wesley was not concerned with an abstract "orthodoxy." His concern was for a lived "orthodoxy."[8]

In practice this can be seen in the revival. The only question persons had to answer to become members of a class was the classic question, "Do you desire to flee from the wrath to come?" Of course, they had to give evidence of the sincerity of their answer by the conduct of their lives. Once in the classes, doctrine became a matter of serious import, not that it was taught didactically (such instruction in doctrine was one function of the society), but the class meetings were in essence sessions where the participants plotted out their spiritual journey to date in terms of the ordering of grace. How goes it with your soul tonight? Are you struggling with a sense of guilt and inadequacy? In other words, are you under the conviction of your sins? Are you under prevenient grace? Or have you received the word of forgiveness and pardon? Have you experienced the gracious liberty of sin forgiven? Are you in justifying grace? Or, again, are you earnestly seeking a fuller Christian life? Are you seeking the empowerment of the Spirit? Are you in sanctifying grace? On the surface, the questions prescribed for the classes may sound somewhat legalistic. But seen within the perspective of the purpose of the classes (to bring persons to Christ and to keep them with Christ), these questions endeavored to probe where a person was in the journey of grace. The role of right doctrine for Wesleyans has rarely been a juridical one, determining who is in and who is out. The primary role of right doctrine for Wesleyans is the formation of a grace-ful, Christian character.

That "vital orthodoxy" practiced by the societies and classes is clearly illustrated by one of Wesley's laywomen, who without the benefits of formal theological training other than the class and society meetings, was able, to make a very discerning doctrinal distinction, both experientially and cognitively.

I Am A Sinner, Saved Freely By Grace:
Grace, divine grace is worthy to have all the glory. Some people I have heard speak much of our faithfulness: I never could bear this; it is GOD'S FAITHFULNESS to his own word of promise, that is my only security for salvation.[9]

Wesley's expectation of his people to be a thinking people speaks to an evangelism that is so preoccupied with methods as to forget the content. Our contemporary problem in getting the church into an evangelistic mode is not simply that we have forgotten how to witness; we have forgotten why we witness. And that is a theological issue of the first order. Can the church learn to think again, rather than hanker for what we call "relevance to the contemporary culture"? Too often in the past, we have attempted to get the message out before we have ever bothered to get it straight.

For North American Christians who are serious about reforming the church so that it may become a more faithful bearer of the gospel in our social context, there is no alternative to a disciplined, prolonged, and above all critical work of theology. This is not an appeal for a textbook theology. Much more is required. Our Christendom churches have lived with such close ties with the dominant culture for so long that if there is to be a freeing of the church's cultural captivity so that the church can once again move in mission, only a theological grasp of the faith can critique and cut those cultural ties. Most of our United Methodist Churches could not measure up to the minimal standards of catechesis demanded by Wesley in the eighteenth century!

This is particularly the case with the evangelism dimension of the Christian mission. Evangelism advocates have been long on technique and embarrassingly short on theological thinking. Is it any wonder, then, why the long-time fixation with technique in our time has produced the morally grotesque revelations of television evangelists?

Right Conduct

This has to do with the practice of the Christian faith. If participation in the class meeting was not a matter doctrinal indifference, such participation was likewise not a matter of moral indifference. The moral standards, grounded in scripture and tradition, were the basis for more dismissals from classes and societies than theological deviation! By the moral witness, supported by the disciplines of spiritual exercise, and the corporate worship of the people, the early Methodists demonstrated again and again that their words of witness were persuasively credible when people saw the lives they lived. What is said of individual moral witness applies equally to the church as corporate moral witness.

Right Passion

Right passion is at the core of "heart religion." Wesley wrote of "experimental" religion, and by this he meant "experiential religion." The experience of justifying faith brought peace and joy to the believer. The experience was not of generic peace or generic joy; it wasn't just any peaceful sentiment or any joyful emotion. The experience was specific. Christian peace is the peace of God that comes with a new right-wised relationship established by God's action in Christ. Christian joy is the specific joy of sins forgiven.

The Christian church today is rediscovering the experiential. Much of experiential worship is authentic, but careful to avoid uncritical psychologistic emotionalism. Wesley was certainly acquainted with some forms of enthusiasm in his day that he critiqued and found wanting. How do we critique the claims and evidences of passion? Wesley knew of only two tests: (1) Is it doctrinally sound? And (2) is it accompanied with the "fruits of the Spirit"? Wesley would remind us that true Christian joy is rooted in the confession of our sin and the subsequent peace of forgiveness.[10]

The year is 1739. We have been blessed with a precious legacy, not to be neglected, hoarded, or frozen into a Wesleyan legalism. Wesley was no alabaster saint. His ways were greatly shaped by his times. But he was a mighty ambassador, neither for himself nor for his people, but for Christ in a world that God in Christ has so loved. What more could God ask of an ambassador?

> See how great a flame aspires,
> kindled by a spark of grace.
> Jesus' love the nations fires,
> sets the kingdoms on a blaze.
> To bring fire on earth he came,
> kindled in some hearts it is;
> O that all might catch the flame,
> all partake the glorious bliss!
>
> When he first the work begun,
> small and feeble was his day;
> Now the Word doth swiftly run,
> now it wins its widening way;
> more and more it spreads and grows,
> ever mighty to prevail;
> sin's strongholds it now o'er-throws,
> shakes the trembling gates of hell.

Saints of God, your Savior praise,
  who the door hath opened wide;
he hath given the word of grace,
  Jesus' word is glorified;
Jesus mighty to redeem,
  who alone the work hath wrought;
worthy is the work of him,
  him who spake a world from naught.

Saw ye not the cloud arise,
  little as a human hand?
Now it spreads along the skies,
  hangs o'er all the thirsty land.
Lo! The promise of a shower
  drops already from above;
but the Lord will shortly pour
  all the spirit of his love.[11]

Discussion Questions

1. How does our contemporary culture differ from the culture of Christendom described by the author?

2. With regard to evangelism, what are the implications of living in the mission field of "a neo-pagan north America"?

3. List the six "bad habits" mentioned in the chapter. Have any of those bad habits surfaced in your local church? If yes, what new habits might your congregation begin to practice in their place?

4. Brainstorm for a moment. How differently would you and your local church act if Christians functioned primarily as a "sent people"?

NOTES

1. Alfred Krass, *Evangelizing Neopagan North America* (Scottsdale, PA: Herald Press, 1992).

2. Kennon Callahan, *New Beginnings for Pastors and Congregations* (San Francisco, CA: Jossey Bass, 1999).

3. S. T. Kimbrough, *Resistless Love* (New York: General Board of Global Ministries, The United Methodist Church, 1998).

4. David J. Bosch, *Transforming Mission: Paradigm Shifts in Theology of Mission* (Maryknoll, NY: Orbis Books, 2001).

5. See Rodney Clapp, *A Peculiar People: The Church as Culture in a Post- Christian Society* (Downers Grove, IL: InterVarsity Press, 1996).

6. Peter Berger, *The Sacred Canopy: Elements of a Sociological Theory of Religion* (Garden City, NY: Anchor Books, 1969).

7. Richard Steele, *"Heart Religion" in the Methodist Tradition and Related* Movements (Lanham, MD: Scarecrow Press, 2001).

8. See the extraordinarily perceptive essay by Randy Maddox, "Vital Orthodoxy: A Wesleyan Dynamic for 21st Century Christianity," in *Methodist History* (Oct. 2001), 3-19.

9.William Bennet, *Memoirs of Mrs. Grace Bennet* (Macclesfield: Printered and sold by E. Bayler, 1803, 83, as quoted in Paul Wesley Chilcote, *Her Own Story: Autobiographical Portraits of Early Methodist Women* (Nashville: Kingswood Books, 2001), 25.

10. I am gratefully endebted to Richard Steel's delineation of these three Wesleyan dynamics in the life of faith personally and corporately.

11. Charles Wesley's hymn on the revival written in 1749. See *The United Methodist Hymnal*

Bibliography

Primary sources

Bicentennial Edition of the Works of John Wesley (Nashville:
  Abingdon Press, 1975).
Letters of the Rev. John Wesley, 8 vols., ed. J. Telford
  (London: Epworth Press 1865; Fourth ed,
  Tentmaker, 1998).

Secondary sources

Bennet, William. *Memoirs of Mrs. Grace* Bennet
  (Macclesfield: Printed and sold by E. Bayler, 1803.
Berger, Peter. *The Sacred Canopy: Elements in a Sociology of
  Religion* (Garden City: NY: Anchor Books, 1969).
Bosch, David. *Transforming Mission: Paradigm Shifts in
  Theology of Mission* Maryknoll, NY: Orbis Books,
  2000).
Chilcote, Paul Wesley. *John Wesley and the Women
  Preachers of Early Methodism* (Metuchen, NJ:
  Scarecrow Press, Inc., 1991).
Clapp, Rodney. *A Peculiar People: The Church as Culture
  in a Post-Christian Society* Downers Grove, IL:
  InterVarsity Press, 1996).
Edwards, Maldwy, *My Dear Sister: The Story of John
  Wesley and the Women in His Life* (Manchester:
  Periwork (Leeds), n.d.).
Fitzgerald, W. B. *The Roots of Methodism* ((London:
  Charles H. Kelly, 1903).
Gruder, Darrell. *The Continuing Conversion of the Church*
  (Grand Rapids, MI: W. B. Eerdmans, 2000).

Kimbrough, S. T., Jr. *Resistless Love* (New York: General Board of Global Ministries, The United Methodist Church, 1998).

Knox, Ronald A. *Enthusiasm* (Oxford: Oxford University Press, 1950).

Krass, Alfred. *Evangelizing Neopagan North America* (Scottsdale, PA: Herald Press, 1992.).

Laycock, J. W., *Methodist and Heroes of the Great Haworth Round, 1734-1784* (Keighsey: Wadsworth, Rydal Press, 1909).

Logan, James C. "Free Grace: Wesley's theology and the Calvinist Challenge," in *Virginia United Methodist Heritage*, XXIX 2 (Fall 2003), pp. 21-31.

——————, "The Evangelical Imperative: A Wesleyan Perspective," in *Theology Evangelism in the Wesleyan Heritage* (Nashville: Kingswood Books, 1994).

Maddox, Randy. *Responsible Grace: John Wesley's Practical Theology* (Nashville: Kingswood Books, 1994).

——————, "Vital Orthodoxy: A Wesleyan Dynamic for the 21st Century," in *Methodist History* (Oct. 2001), pp. 3-19.

Outler, Albert. *Evangelism in the Wesleyan Spirit* (Nashville: Tidings, 1974).

Pilkington, W. *The Makers of Wesleyan Methodism in Preston* (London: Charles H. Kelly, 1890).

Richardson, W. F. *Preston Methodism's Two Hundred Years* (Preston: Printed at Adelphi Chambers by Henry L. Kirby 1975).

Steele, Richard, ed. *"Heart Religion" in the Methodist Tradition and Related Movements* (Lanham, MD: Scarecrow Press, 2001).

Taylor, John. *The Apostles of Fylde Methodism* (London: T. Woolman, 1885).

Turner, John Munsey, *John Wesley: The Evangelical Revival and the Rise of Methodism in England* (Peterborough: Epworth Press, 2002).

About the Author

The Rev. Dr. James C. Logan (1932-2009)

Dr. James C. Logan was Professor of Systematic Theology at Wesley Theological Seminary from 1966 until 1990. In 1990, he was installed as the first E. Stanley Jones Professor of Evangelism at Wesley. He served in that position until his retirement in 2001. He earned his A.B. from Florida Southern College, his S.T.B. from Boston University School of Theology, and his Ph.D. from Boston University. He pursued doctoral and post-doctoral studies at Harvard University; St. Mary's College, University of St. Andrews, Scotland; University of Basel, Switzerland; and the University of Cambridge, England. In 1986, he received the Alumni Distinguished Service Award from Florida Southern College.

Dr. Logan was an ordained minister of The United Methodist Church. After his studies at Boston University, he served as Associate Pastor at Hyde Park

Community Methodist Church in Cincinnati, OH. In 1964, he transferred his membership to the Holston Conference and served for two years as Assistant Professor of Religion and Philosophy and Pastor of the Campus Church at Emory and Henry College, Emory Virginia.

Dr. Logan transferred to the Virginia Annual Conference in 1977. Seven times he was elected a delegate to the quadrennial General Conference of The United Methodist Church, serving as chair of the clergy delegation five times. He was a director of the General Board of Global Ministries of The United Methodist Church and was a member of the World Methodist Council. He was the author of five books in theology. When Dr. Logan was installed as E. Stanley Jones Professor of Evangelism in 1995, Bishop Earl G. Hunt, Jr., President of the Foundation for Evangelism that created the professorship, stated: "The Foundation is delighted that James Cecil Logan, one of United Methodism's brilliant minds and a highly respected, greatly beloved scholar and minister, has been chosen for this professorship."

In 1999, the Foundation for Evangelism named Dr. Logan as the 1999 Denman Distinguished Evangelist and Wesley Theological Seminary established the James C. Logan Chair in Evangelism in his honor. At that time, Dr. Logan stated:

"Evangelism is not an optional activity of the church; it is an expression of the church's very being and mission."

[Printed with permission of The Southwest Times, Pulaski, Virginia.]